# Transcending Change

## Inspiring sayings for testing transitions

CONTROLLAH GABI

TRANSCENDING CHANGE

Published by Altralogue
124 City Road
London
United Kingdom
EC1V 2NX
www.altralogue.com

Zimbabwe
Altralogue PL
Harare & Bindura

First published in the USA & United Kingdom in 2023

Copyright © 2023 Controllah Gabi

All rights are reserved. No part of this publication may be reproduced, stored in a retrieval system, or transmitted in any form or by any means, electronic, mechanical, photocopying, recording or otherwise, without prior permission of the Author. For permissions and enquiries, contact:
Controllah@hotmail.co.uk
Twitter: @DrContieGabi
LinkedIn:
https://uk.linkedin.com/in/controllahgabi

ISBN: 978-1-9993034-7-1

# DEDICATION

Kuna Baba vangu, VaFreeborn Gabi. I draw strength from your unwavering commitment to your calling to take care of us through the taxing times of colonial and post-colonial Zimbabwe. You never stopped caring.

# CONTENTS

| | |
|---|---|
| ACKNOWLEDGMENTS | i |
| EMBRACING CHANGE AS A PERSONAL JOURNEY | 1 |
| SHIFTING PERSPECTIVES | 8 |
| GROWING THROUGH CHANGE | 16 |
| SEIZING NEW OPPORTUNITIES | 21 |
| ACTIVE ENGAGEMENT | 24 |
| ADAPTING TO THE UNPREDICTABLE | 31 |
| OVERCOMING FEAR OF CHANGE | 35 |
| THE POWER OF CURIOSITY | 40 |
| LEARNING FROM MISTAKES | 43 |
| THE JOURNEY OF INNOVATION | 46 |

# ACKNOWLEDGMENTS

Josie, for being ever present.

# EMBRACING CHANGE AS A PERSONAL JOURNEY

Change is an ever present constant in life. It can be unsettling and disruptive. It is an uncertain time, and you don't know what the future holds for you. This uncertainty breeds excitement, trepidation and fear – a tension of emotions contradicting each other. You may have others to lend support, but one thing clear – this change is about you. It is a personal journey where only you are having direct interaction with it. It is good that it is personal; this gives you the power to make the important calls. Here are some words for reassurance, motivation, and guidance.

When I was born, I signed up for change. It's a lifelong subscription.

This is my moment; my life has been preparing me for this.

I will start this journey as I should, seeing the destination I want.

I'll face this my way as I'm experiencing it my way.

I love myself too much to let myself down.


I'll confront this as if my life depends on it, because it does.


Change is when you get to learn a lot about yourself you didn't know. Like all lessons in life, make the most of it.

Being alone at this hour may not be the worst that could happen; it is the rare moment when all noise and distraction is shut out to let you be yourself and figure out what the hell you want out of life and go for it.


This is change is for me, I'm up for it.


Change is my shadow; it comes in my shape and follows me everywhere.

There is only one person who matters in this. Me!

I have come so far; I can't remember how to go back; so, I move forward.

I'm glad I have the most important person by my side at this moment, someone who's always been there by my side. Me.

Change is my very nature; I inhale it and exhale it in order to stay alive. It is my life. It is me. I'm the change.

This may slow you down, but never let it stop you.

No one prepares you for change better than you.

Don't waste time yearning for those who have deserted you during this change; they were not meant to be here.

No one is more committed to your cause than you. Count on yourself to serve your best interests.

Remember how you felt when you started this and keep going; you have travelled too far to give up.

## SHIFTING PERSPECTIVES

How you view a transition matters as it determines how you deal with it and how you feel. It reflects and affects your attitude which, in turn, impacts your confidence and the action you take. Times of difficult change are times for strategizing, not for worrying.

When you stop feeling, you'll start thinking.

If you hate change, you don't understand life and existence.

I will stop feeling and start thinking.

You can't hate change and want to benefit from it.

At this very moment, someone is being born; someone is graduating; someone is getting married; someone has missed their flight; someone is kissing. This is just a moment in time; it's not a big as it feels.

The adventurous live a life of fulfilment not because of who they are, but because they change with change often enough to become one with change.

Like gold, at some point you've got to go through the hottest furnace for your finest self to emerge.

Who can change without change?

Only those who don't perceive see change as an enemy.

Where would I be without change?

Besides change, what other options do you have?

Feeling pain is a sign of life. Manage it, don't ignore it.

The joy of a new life follows the travail of labour.

The best things in life come at the highest cost; if costs that much, it has the highest value.

Even the finest gold goes through the hottest fire; when it emerges in purity, only its quality knows what it's been through. Only those who can afford it will pay whatever it takes to have it.

Before it's over, it feels eternal; when it's over, you'll realise it was temporary.

As victory exists because of war, healing exists because of pain.

If despair hurts, try hope.

A shadow is proof of light.

It's over not because you failed, but because you saw it through.

Only those standing stagger; every step they make doesn't care about the rhythm of their walk.
A hurting heart is a beating heart; draw life from it.

When a key hasn't unlocked a door, there's nothing wrong with the key; it's just the wrong door.

## GROWING THROUGH CHANGE

Growth itself is change, and change is a growth point. Without change, there is no growth. If handled properly and with the right attitude, times of change can be growth transitions. This is not the first time you are facing difficult change in your life. Remember how you have shown resilience and grown through past experiences. As were those past transitions, every change is an opportunity for personal development. This moment may feel different, but the same qualities that have seen you through past difficulties will help you navigate through this.

I have always grown through change.

Ask yourself, what can I learn from this and learn and grow.

A change you can't change requires you to change.

Change is your runway; gain your lift from it. Soon you'll be flying above the clouds.

If things go wrong, I will learn and grow.

Resilience is borne out of adversity.

When they said I would never do it, I knew it was time for change.

If your network can't change you, change your network.

Don't get married to someone like you; it's like marrying yourself. A change marriage is marrying someone who complements you. That person completes you - they make you whole, and your journey towards change begins.

Now is the time to put the lessons you've learnt in your life to work.

The pain of failure should spur you to avoid it.

Life doesn't come with a manual; experience gives the most valuable instructions for how to live it. Learn from your situation and will have a manual for it.

## SEIZING NEW OPPORTUNITIES

It may not feel like it, but every change brings new opportunities and a chance to gain new skills. However, not everything is completely new; your existing skills and knowledge will still be relevant. Just consider leveraging these skills and knowledge in new, innovative ways.

This is the beginning of a new opportunity.

This is a new season requiring new skills.

This is an opportunity for me to use my existing skills and knowledge in new ways.

This is the moment my life has been preparing me for.

I'm about to gain new skills and acquire new insights.

Change comes in types; each type is once-in-a-lifetime - when it's gone, it's gone. Look for the advantage and take advantage of it.

This is the flood that floats my boat.

## ACTIVE ENGAGEMENT

A time of change is not a time to be passive and leave your life to fate. It is a time to summon energy and courage and be proactive. Engaging with change gives you a sense of agency and puts you in control. Engagement is empowering and inspiring. You become the force behind your fate. Rather than being a passive spectator, use the time of change to reflect, strategize, and act.

A time of change is not a time to be passive; it is a time for thinking, for reflection, for strategizing, for leveraging, for action. It's a time to be fully attuned.

Make change your friend, not your enemy. Like a friend, learn what it is like, understand what it requires and start adapting to it enough for you to be great buddies with it.

I will run towards change,
not away from it.


I will affect how this change
affects me.


I will not passively let this
change do things to me; I will
engage with it for the best
outcome.


In the change game, those
who dictate it win.

Great wars are not won in familiar battles and familiar surroundings; to win you've got to deal with change, deal with the unknown like you know it, deal with change like you are causing it - being the force, rather than the forced.

You've benefited from change all your life, it's time you participated in it.

Make change your friend, not your foe.

People envy those who change, not those who stay the same.

Only when you begin to change does the world take notice of you. Until then, you don't exist.

Change drivers are the only beings making the news.

Don't just tell yourself, I've got this, when you don't. Moments of change are moments of honesty to yourself. Audit yourself and make necessary adjustments to get out at the other end okay.

Your situation doesn't define you, how you handle it may.

Your career is important, but you are more important.

Shape your career; don't let it shape you.

## ADAPTING TO THE UNPREDICTABLE

Times of change are times of unpredictability. Do not expect familiar things to happen the same way they have in the past with the same patterns and intensities. Expecting the unexpected and anticipating things that may surprise you puts you in the right preparedness for responding to unknowns. You become adaptable and resilient.

Without discomfort, there can be no change.

Don't dim. Shine.

I'm done being the same, doing the same, the same way. It's time for a change!

When I started this, I had noble goals; I'll keep fighting for them, adapting my strategy as change happens.

Like Noah's ark, the flood that drowned others will float my boat - because life has prepared me for this.

Stay the same and go stale.

Things which are always the same are boring; they lack the excitement and sense of adventure.

Don't blur. Perceive.

Moments of change are moments of adjustments.

When the time of change comes, figure out adjustments you need to make, and make them.

## OVERCOMING FEAR OF CHANGE

Fear is a normal reaction to change. It comes from a sudden sense of uncertainty and a feeling that you do not have control over what is happening. It is human nature to imagine the worst. However, the worst rarely happens in life and, by now, you will have learned from past experiences that the worst seldomly happened. During times of change, it is important to take care of your personal happiness and sense of satisfaction. Put everything in perspective and consider the big picture. Change is an integral part of life and embracing it leads to fulfillment.

What's the worst that can happen?

I was born to embrace change, not to fear it.

Those who fear change will forever live a miserable life, because life is change and change is life.

This is not going to kill me.

It's not as bad as it feels. Imagine the worst that could happen. Imagine the best that could happen. Your reality is somewhere in between. Now, start strategizing for the best outcome.

Worrying about this won't move the needle on my chances of success, planning and acting will.

I saw this coming. The reason why I didn't run away was because I was prepared for it; now is my moment to confront it.

This didn't come earlier in my life because I wasn't ready; now I AM.

The fact that I'm still standing counts.

You're beautiful, but it's the steel in you that'll pull you through.

Darkness gives light its meaning; don't fear it, turn on your light.

## THE POWER OF CURIOSITY

Uncertainty means something is unknown. Rather than trigger fear in you, let this generate curiosity. Curiosity, not fear, is a platform for learning. Learning what this change is, what it means, how it impacts you and ways for navigating it. You also learn a lot about yourself and the journey you have travelled during times of change. If you approach change with an open mind, you will realise your potential for growth and discovery.

Instead of fear, uncertainty should trigger curiosity.

The uncertainty of change is what brings curiosity, and curiosity discovery, and discovery growth. This excitement makes you want to face change again. And again. And again.

In the darkest hour, the faintest light is enough to

keep you going; don't let it go out.

The need to keep going is never more urgent than when you are in an undesirable place; you need to keep going to get out of it. Stopping is never an option as it prolongs the undesirability.

## LEARNING FROM MISTAKES

Some change comes because of a mistake. There is nothing wrong with making a mistake if you learn from it and grow. Yes, mistakes can be painful, but do not dwell on them. Rather, focus on why that mistake happens. All mistakes have one thing in common; they happened because you tried something. Life itself is a big, long trial; we are always trying, occasionally making mistakes. Only those who never try never make mistakes. This is an opportunity to turn mistake to your advantage.

A change that comes from a mistake is the beginning of a journey to improvement.

If this change is happening because of something you didn't do, this is time to do something.

If this change is because of something you did, it's time to do things differently.

This could be when you say NEVER AGAIN and mean it.

The greatest thing after a destruction is not the rubble, it is the rebuilding. Focus on it and the renewal it brings.

## THE JOURNEY OF INNOVATION

This change should not spell the end for you. It should be the birth of a new beginning. Feel the freshness of the breeze of a new dawn. Most great ideas and inventions that changed this world emerged during times of change. They were so compelling, so forceful that they became the change. You may not seek to change the world, but this moment could be a catalyst for a significant turning point in your life. Use this as a catalyst for creative thinking. As well as work for you, the ideas you generate can be inspirational to others too.

Many great ideas, life-changing inventions and technologies started as ideas born in moments of change. Generate yours from this change.

A change from a crisis will not be solved by a crisis of ideas.

Don't dip. Think.

Experiencing darkness led to the invention of light.

You've got a brain for a reason. Use it.

Let this unpleasantness be a springboard for the invention of comfort.

The devil you know makes you complacent; the devil you don't know keeps you honest, keeps you on your toes, keeps your wits about. The devil you don't know is where your innovation lies; that's where your opportunity is.


Don't wait to install airbags in your car after it has crashed. The best change happens when it's not needed; this is the kind of change you initiate, not that which is imposed on you.

You are a product of change; to produce something, initiate a change.


You don't need new tools to deal with this; you need new ways to use the tools you have.

## CLOSING

Change is unsettling and a great source of a sense of anxiousness, uncertainty, self-doubt, excitement, hope and curiosity. These contradicting emotions are what makes change complex and difficult to deal with. However, with an open mind, change can be a force for good regardless of its causes and circumstances. The true nature of change is that it is an opportunity for reflection, growth, development and creativity. Embrace change as a natural part of life that is inevitable. Approach it with courage, confidence and a positive and proactive attitude to take advantage of it. Apply the sayings as affirmations during times of difficulty and transformation.

www.ingramcontent.com/pod-product-compliance
Lightning Source LLC
Chambersburg PA
CBHW041751040426
42446CB00001B/4